DOGS

THE COLORING BOOK

AFGHAN HOUND

AUSTRALIAN SHEPHERD

BASSET HOUND

BEAGLE

BICHON FRISE

BORDER COLLIE

BOSTON TERRIER

BOXER

BULL TERRIER

CAIRN TERRIER

CAVALIER KING CHARLES SPANIEL

CHIHUAHUA

CHINESE CRESTED

CHOW CHOW

COCKER SPANIEL

CORGI

DACHSHUND

DALMATIAN

DOBERMAN PINSCHER

ENGLISH BULLDOG

FRENCH BULLDOG

GERMAN SHEPHERD

GOLDEN DOODLE

GOLDEN RETRIEVER

GREYHOUND

GREAT DANE

JACK RUSSELL

IRISH SETTER

LABRADOR RETRIEVER

MALTESE

MASTIFF

PAPILLON

PITBULL TERRIER

POMERANIAN

POODLE

PUG

ROTTWEILER

ROUGH COLLIE

SAINT BERNARD

SAMOYED

SCHNAUZER

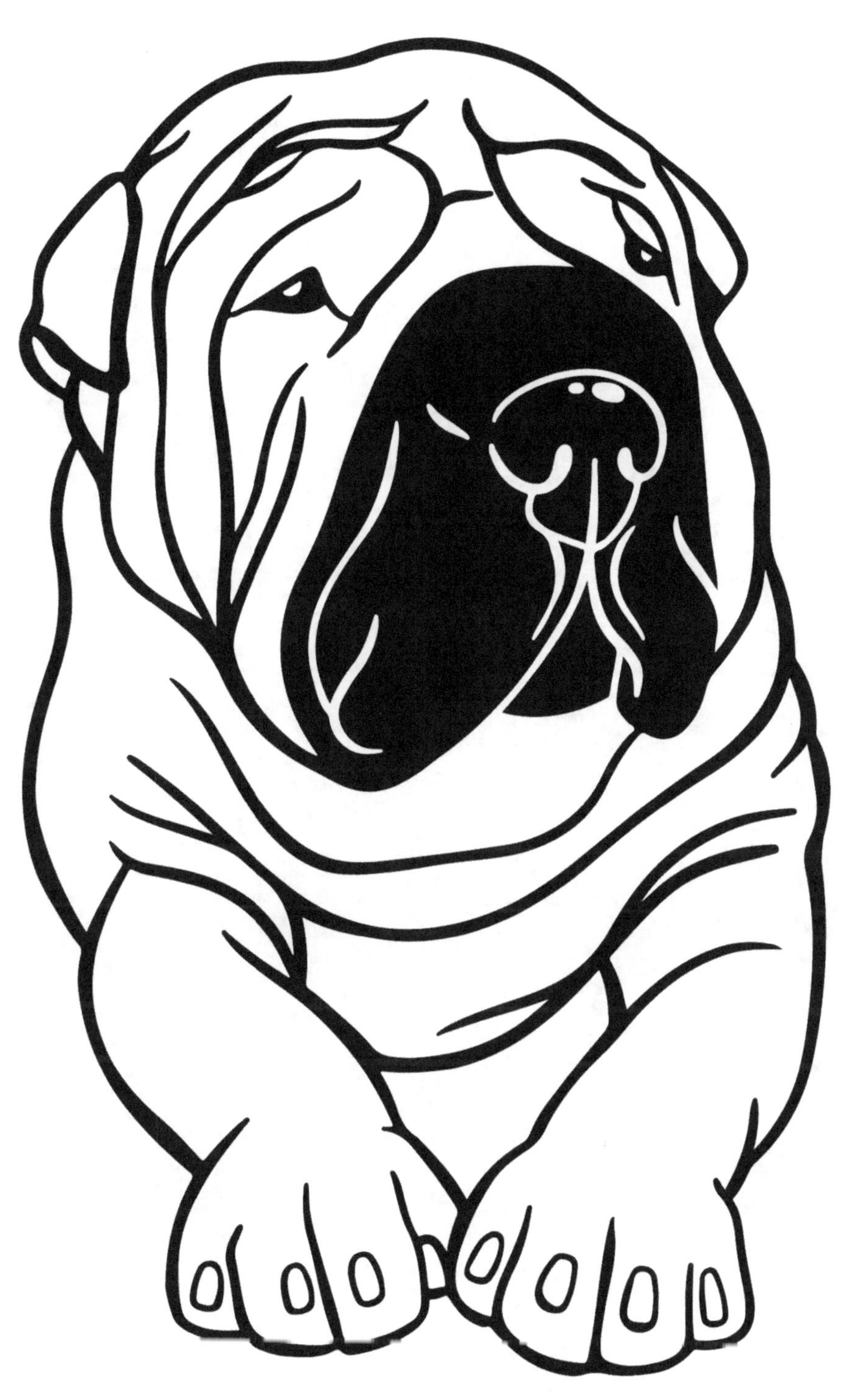

SHAR PEI

SHIBA INU

SHIH TZU

SIBERIAN HUSKY

SILKY TERRIER

TOY POODLE

VIZSLA

WEST HIGHLAND WHITE TERRIER

YORKSHIRE TERRIER